# Giant Pandas

## A Carolrhoda Nature Watch Book

by Lynn M. Stone
photographs by Keren Su

Carolrhoda Books, Inc. / Minneapolis

*For my wife, who encouraged me to study
pandas on their own turf*      —L.M.S.

*To my wife, Cecilia, and my daughter,
Leanne*      —K.S.

Text copyright © 2004 by Lynn M. Stone
Photographs copyright © 2004 by Keren Su
Map on p. 17 by Laura Westlund, copyright © 2004 by
Carolrhoda Books, Inc.

Additional photographs reproduced through the courtesy of
Lynn M. Stone, pp. 15 (right), 19 (bottom), 36.

Carolrhoda Books, Inc.
A division of Lerner Publishing Group
241 First Avenue North
Minneapolis, MN 55401 U.S.A.

Website address: www.lernerbooks.com

Library of Congress Cataloging-in-Publication Data

Stone, Lynn M.
    Giant pandas / by Lynn M. Stone ; photographs by Keren Su.
      p.   cm.
    "A Carolrhoda nature watch book."
    Includes index.
    Contents: Giant pandas — Pandas and bears — Panda country
— The bamboo bear — The panda's neighborhood —
Courtship and cubs — Saving the giant panda.
    ISBN: 1-57505-343-8 (lib. bdg. : alk. paper)
    1. Giant panda—Juvenile literature. 2. Giant panda—
China—Juvenile literature. [1. Giant panda. 2. Pandas.
3. Endangered species.] I. Su, Keren, ill. II. Title.
QL737.C214S76 2004
599.789—dc21
                                                2003010552

Manufactured in the United States of America
1 2 3 4 5 6 – JR – 09 08 07 06 05 04

# CONTENTS

# Giant Pandas

Above: *Giant pandas have distinctive black-and-white markings.*
Opposite page: *A giant panda plays in a tree.*

# GIANT PANDAS

The giant panda is one of the world's most endearing wild animals. It is also one of the rarest. No one knows exactly how many giant pandas remain in the wild. There may be no more than 1,000.

Much of the giant panda's charm arises from its appearance. The giant panda looks much like a child's teddy bear. It has a thick, woolly, black-and-white coat. It has a broad moon face with big, black patches around its eyes and round Mickey Mouse ears. Giant pandas look, well, huggable.

A giant panda is usually a roly-poly, easygoing creature. Few people have seen a giant panda in a big hurry. Still, giant pandas are very entertaining. A panda loves to sprawl on its back or rump. This mass of fur and muscle almost seems to pour itself into a comfortable position. It can make a rock into a sofa. Occasionally a giant panda will stand on its hind legs, looking a bit like a shaggy, masked person.

*A panda sprawls out on the ground.*

*Bamboo plants have stiff stalks* (left) *and long, narrow leaves* (above).

Lolling about comes naturally for giant pandas. They are active for about 12 to 14 hours each day, and they spend most of that time eating. About 99 percent of a panda's diet consists of **bamboo,** a hard-stemmed grass. Pandas eat the sprouts, stems, and leaves of bamboo plants.

A panda finds a stand of bamboo, hunkers down, and starts eating. It does not stand on all fours, **muzzle** down, like a grizzly bear grazing in a pasture. Instead, the panda eats sitting upright or sprawled out, using its forepaws like hands. A panda pops a stalk of bamboo into its mouth as casually as you would pop a pretzel into yours.

In China, where wild pandas live, people have many nicknames for the giant panda. Some call it the "bamboo bear." The name fits, because the panda is as dependent on bamboo as a cow is on grass.

The giant panda is a popular subject for Chinese artists.

For the Chinese, the giant panda is a national treasure. The panda has fascinated the Chinese people for centuries. A panda was mentioned in a collection of Chinese poetry, the *Shi Jing,* written some 3,000 years ago. A Chinese dictionary written 2,200 years ago described the panda as a "bamboo-eating leopard with black and white markings." Even in modern times, many Chinese people compare pandas to cats. A common Chinese name for the giant panda, *da xiongmao* (dah-shung-mah-ow), translates to "large bear cat."

Although the Chinese have known the giant panda for centuries, the Western world of Europe and the Americas have known of it only since 1869. Père (Father) Armand David, a French missionary, was the first to bring news of the giant panda's existence to the West. Père David brought skins and bones of giant pandas to France in 1869. In 1929, two Americans were apparently the first Westerners to see a live panda. That brief encounter ended with the two men shooting the animal for a museum collection. The first living pandas to be exhibited in the United States arrived at Chicago's Brookfield Zoo in 1936.

Even in more recent years, few people have seen pandas in the wild. But millions of people have seen giant pandas in the few zoos where they are shown. Such exhibits kindle great affection for these rare bears.

*Giant pandas walk on all fours, like other bears. The giant panda's scientific name is* Ailuropoda melanoleuca, *which means "black-and-white cat-footed one."*

# PANDAS AND BEARS

Père David introduced a wonderful "new" animal to much of the world. He also stirred a debate among **taxonomists.** Taxonomists are scientists who study how an animal is put together. Then they decide into which group of animals it should be placed, such as meat eater or plant eater, cat or dog.

Usually, our common names for animals result from what the taxonomists have learned. For example, the common name *white-tailed deer* refers to one of several kinds of deer. But even taxono-mists struggled with what the giant panda was. None of them thought that the panda was a leopard or any other kind of cat. But the taxonomists could not agree, scientifically speaking, on just what the panda *was.*

Some scientists believed from the beginning of the debate, more than 100 years ago, that the giant panda was a bear. It had the stocky build, small eyes, shaggy fur, and shuffling walk of bears. A bear, to be sure, they said.

*Unlike most bears, giant pandas do not hibernate in the winter.*

Other scientists argued that the giant panda was a bear in appearance only. They pointed out that the giant panda almost never eats meat. Other bears regularly eat meat for at least part of their diet. Most bear species **hibernate,** too, except those living in the warmest areas of the earth. Giant pandas live in cool, **temperate** forests, but they do not hibernate. And what about the panda's voice? Giant pandas make many sounds, from bleats and chirps to squeals, moans, and barks. But they rarely roar. Real bears, the doubters said, growl and roar a whole lot.

The non-bear group had still more ammunition. Some of the bones and teeth of the giant panda, they said, are more like those of raccoons and the smaller red panda than they are like those of bears. Furthermore, they argued, the giant panda has unique handlike forepaws. The panda has an extension of one of its wrist bones that gives it a sixth **digit,** or finger. The sixth digit works like a thumb. It permits the panda to use its forepaws with great agility. A panda grips bamboo by locking it between this nimble "thumb" and the rest of its paw. No other bear has a sixth digit.

The taxonomists fell into three main groups. Group one said the giant panda belonged with raccoons and the red panda. Group two thought the giant panda should be in a family by itself. Group three said the panda was a bear.

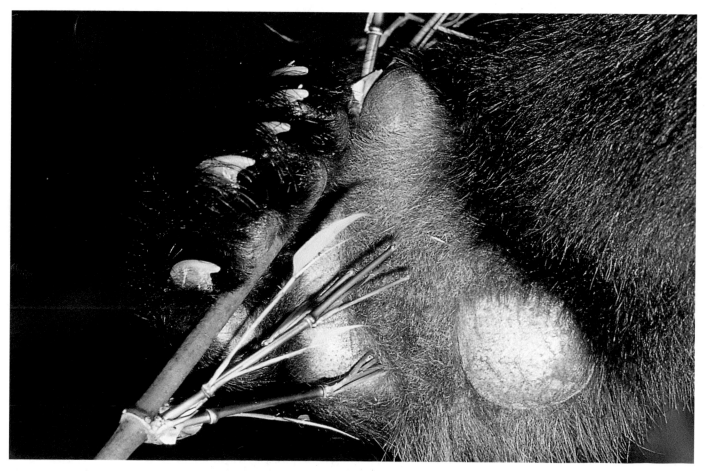

*A giant panda's front paw has five digits with claws, plus a wrist bone that works like a thumb.*

*The red, or lesser, panda is a member of the raccoon family.*

For most authorities, the issue was settled in the mid-1990s, when scientists studied giant panda **DNA.** DNA is the material in the cells of living things that can pass characteristics from parents to their offspring. Scientists compared the DNA of giant pandas to the DNA of raccoons, red pandas, and bears. The studies showed that giant pandas are, indeed, bears, even if they are most unusual bears.

The DNA studies also showed that the red panda is *not* a bear. The long-tailed red, or lesser, panda is much smaller than the giant panda. The red panda rarely weighs more than 12 pounds (5.5 kg). It is a member of the raccoon family, rather than the bear family. The red panda does, however, have some kinship with the giant panda. Like giant pandas, red pandas have a small "thumb" on their forepaws and broad, flat side teeth. Red pandas also eat bamboo, although they eat roots, acorns, fruits, young birds, and rodents too. Like the giant panda, the red panda is **endangered.** The remaining red pandas live scattered through Nepal, Sikkim, Bhutan, Burma, and parts of China. They share some of the giant panda's range in Sichuan Province, China. But red pandas tend to live higher in the mountains than giant pandas.

Adult male giant pandas weigh 190 to 275 pounds (85–125 kg) and measure up to 6 feet (nearly 2 m) tall when standing on their hind legs. Females weigh 150 to 220 pounds (70–100 kg) and are shorter than males. Males have wider muzzles and stronger forelegs than females.

Although the giant panda is large, it is not a giant among the bears of the world. The biggest bears are the Kodiak brown bears that live on certain islands off the coast of Alaska. These bears may weigh nearly 2,000 pounds (900 kg) and stand over 10 feet (3 m) tall. They are the biggest meat-eating land animals on earth, although, like most bears, they do not live entirely on meat. The giant panda is nowhere near the size of a polar bear, either. Polar bears are nearly as big as Kodiak brown bears. The giant panda is about the same size as the spectacled bear of South America and the sloth bear of Asia. Giant pandas are larger, on the average, than the Asiatic black bears that live in panda country.

**Above:** *Like other bears, giant pandas sometimes stand up on their hind legs.*
**Right:** *Alaska's brown bears grow to be nearly twice as tall as giant pandas.*

# PANDA COUNTRY

Giant pandas live in Sichuan, Gansu, and Shaanxi Provinces in southwestern China, along the eastern edge of the Tibetan plateau. They live in six fairly remote, mountainous regions: the Qinling Mountains in Shaanxi Province, the Min Mountains along the Gansu-Sichuan border, a portion of the Qionglai Mountains in western Sichuan, and the Liang, DaXiang, and Xiao Xiang Mountains in southern Sichuan. By early in the twenty-first century, 35 **reserves,** or places where giant pandas are protected, had been established within these mountain ranges.

It is thought that giant pandas live in roughly 10,000 square miles (26,000 sq. km) of land. The government has protected about half of that in reserves. That may sound like a lot of space for giant pandas. Unfortunately, it is not. It is only a sliver of the more than 300,000 square miles (nearly 800,000 sq. km) where pandas once lived.

*Wolong Valley, Sichuan, China*

16

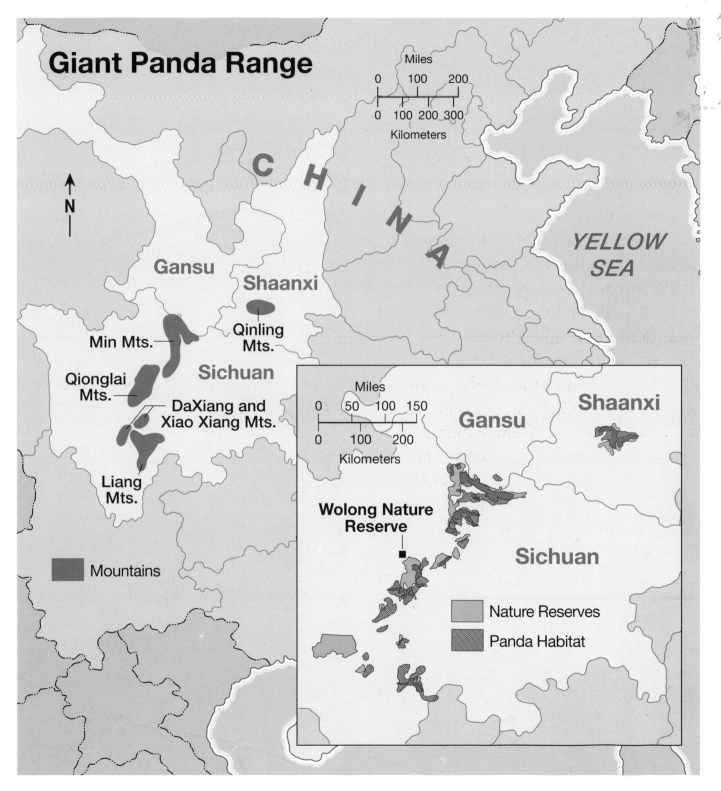

# Giant Panda Range

Miles
0    100    200

0  100  200  300
Kilometers

N

C H I N A

YELLOW
SEA

Gansu

Shaanxi

Min Mts.

Qinling
Mts.

Qionglai
Mts.

Sichuan

DaXiang and
Xiao Xiang Mts.

Liang
Mts.

Mountains

Miles
0    50    100    150

0    100    200
Kilometers

Gansu

Shaanxi

Wolong Nature
Reserve

Sichuan

Nature Reserves

Panda Habitat

Within the mountains and valleys of the Tibetan plateau, giant pandas live in their preferred **habitat.** A habitat is the particular natural community that best meets an animal's specific needs. The giant panda's habitat is mountain forests where bamboo is plentiful and the climate is neither hot nor bitterly cold.

The giant panda's forest home is much like the lush forests of the southern parts of North America's Appalachian Mountains. The Chinese forests and the Appalachians share a green, rugged beauty and a rich assortment of plants and animals. Chinese wildlife is notoriously uncommon. It has been exploited for food, traditional medicine, and fur. But some of the mountain areas where giant pandas survive are also home to leopards, golden cats, Asiatic black bears, golden monkeys, magpies, golden pheasants, red pandas, yellow-throated martens, and the oxlike takin.

*An Asiatic black bear cub*

18

*Other neighbors of the giant panda include the golden pheasant* (left), *the golden monkey* (above left), *and the takin* (above).

19

*Low clouds often surround the giant panda's mountain home.*

The forests where pandas live march from steep slopes down into moist valleys. Above the valleys, mist encircles mountain peaks and hangs among the trees. A few of the most remarkable forests are old-growth forests, or forests whose trees have never been cut. Many old-growth trees are covered by green wisps of **lichens,** or plants that look like dry moss. Tumbling brooks gurgle through the pandas' home and spill into plunging waterfalls. At lower **elevations,** or heights above sea level, pandas pad through forests of broad-leafed trees, such as birch and maple, mixed with evergreens. Gnarly thickets of rhododendron and bamboo rise from a carpet of leaves and ferns. At higher elevations, the forests become more evergreen, dominated by firs and spruces.

Pandas grip tree trunks with their long claws and climb fairly well, although somewhat clumsily. Pandas may climb a tree during courtship or to take a nap in the branches. They may also climb if frightened. Young pandas sometimes seem to climb just for the fun of it.

**Above:** *The giant panda's habitat is lush and green.*
**Right:** *Young pandas often play in trees.*

The season of the year and the abundance of bamboo influence the elevation at which a giant panda lives. Giant pandas live high in the mountains in the summer. They move to lower elevations for the winter. Although high mountain bamboo remains green and edible all winter, pandas seek milder temperatures. They have relatively little body fat to protect them from cold or to act as a food reserve. A panda, like any **mammal,** has to burn more calories to maintain its body heat in cold weather. If it can stay in fairly mild temperatures, the panda needs less food because it uses less energy to keep warm. During the summer, pandas move up the mountains as much as 1 mile (1.6 km) to follow sprouting bamboo.

Giant pandas usually live at an elevation between 8,500 and 9,800 feet (2,600–3,000 m) above sea level. But they live at elevations up to at least 11,500 feet (3,510 m) above sea level in summer. That is about as high as bamboo grows. Giant pandas live at elevations as low as 4,000 feet (1,200 m) above sea level in winter. What was once fine habitat for pandas at even lower elevations has been made into farms and villages.

**This page and opposite:** *The passing seasons bring dramatic color changes in the giant panda's habitat.*

The seasons in these mountains pass with quiet changes of light and color. With the lengthening days of spring, purple and yellow flowers bloom among new-green leaves. In summer, the mountain forests are a canvas of dark green, torn only by rocky outcrops, white plumes of falling water, and the scars where trees have been cut down. Red and gold leaves paint the forests in autumn, before winter snows transform the landscape once again. But it is not beauty that brings the giant panda to the forest. It is the bamboo, nurtured by the damp, chilly air under the forest's trees.

# THE BAMBOO BEAR

Giant pandas depend upon their habitat for safety, water, and food. For a panda, food almost always means bamboo—for breakfast, lunch, dinner, and snacks.

Fortunately, bamboo is plentiful. It comes in several **species,** or kinds. For a panda, with its handy forepaws, plucking bamboo comes naturally. Giant pandas are not particularly fussy about which kind of bamboo they devour. They have been known to consume at least 30 different species. They eat all parts of the bamboo. But they prefer the most nutritious—and probably the tastiest—parts: the green, juicy shoots of new bamboo plants. Shoots are not always available,

however. From April to June, pandas feed mostly on old stems. Between July and October, they largely eat bamboo leaves. Leaves and young stems form the bulk of their diet between November and March.

Over time, the giant panda has adapted to become a bamboo eater. One adaptation is the panda's short muzzle, which has muscles and teeth designed for crushing and chewing. The giant panda's side and back teeth are broad and flat, much like those of grazing animals. The panda's tough throat lining protects it from splinters that its teeth might have missed. The panda's intestines, too, are especially thick walled.

Bamboo is not nutritious, like broccoli is. Even the healthiest parts of bamboo plants are not full of vitamins or even calories. That is a problem for an animal that depends upon eating bamboo.

The panda faces another problem. Its digestive system isn't designed for eating mostly plants. Most plant eaters, like deer and cattle, have a long digestive tract because it takes a lot of effort to break down plant tissues. Bears and other **carnivores,** or meat-eating animals, have a short digestive tract. A meat eater's gut is not long enough to digest plant tissues completely.

To make up for the lack of nutrition in bamboo and the ineffectiveness of the panda's short digestive tract, nature has given the panda a whopping appetite. Giant pandas are bamboo-eating machines. A 220-pound (100-kg) giant panda eats 25 to 30 pounds (11–14 kg) of bamboo stems and leaves in a day. A panda may eat more than 80 pounds (nearly 40 kg) of bamboo shoots in a day. That is nearly 40 percent of the panda's body weight! If you weigh 80 pounds (36 kg), can you imagine gorging yourself on 32 pounds (15 kg) of greens in a day? But an adult panda eating 80 pounds (36 kg) of bamboo does not gain weight, much less become fat. It takes huge quantities of bamboo for a panda to just stay at the same weight.

**Opposite page:** *The giant panda's main food is bamboo, which stays green even in the winter* (inset). **Above:** *Pandas spend most of the day eating.*

Bamboo is usually abundant. But every few years, huge tracts of bamboo in one area or another flower. After they bloom, they die off, leaving pandas without their basic food. These die-offs are called **bamboo crashes.** Some pandas— no one knows how many—have starved as a result of bamboo crashes, such as those that took place in 1974 and 1983.

Not all bamboo species flower and crash at once. So at one time, giant pandas could find at least some tasty species of bamboo alive at any season. A panda deprived of one species, such as arrow bamboo, could wander about until it found another species, such as umbrella bamboo. But pandas have less habitat than they once had. It is harder for some pandas to find other kinds of bamboo during a crash. A panda might once have had to travel only a short distance to find fresh bamboo. But that is no longer the case for some pandas. Beyond a small area of good habitat may lie farms, villages, fields, and roads. In those circumstances, pandas may be unable to find bamboo to eat.

*When bamboo dies off in one area, pandas must travel to find more food.*

*Although giant pandas eat mostly bamboo, their teeth are like those of bears that eat both meat and plants.*

Besides bamboo, giant pandas occasionally eat grass, farm crops, crocuses, irises, and other plants. And very rarely, giant pandas eat meat.

Giant pandas have the long, sharp canine teeth typical of bears and other carnivores. They have the ability to eat meat, and they apparently enjoy it. One team of Chinese researchers who studied wild pandas in the 1980s had some success in using goat meat to lure pandas into traps. Even though meat was not a "natural" food for the pandas, they were apparently drawn by its scent. Like other bears, giant pandas have a keen sense of smell.

Wild giant pandas occasionally consume meat by eating dead animals, or **carrion.** And sometimes they catch small mountain creatures. Like any big, wild animal with sharp teeth and claws, a panda can be dangerous. But despite their teeth, pandas are not **predators,** or hunters. Pandas do not have to hunt, since bamboo does not run. A panda does not have to be fast or sneaky to obtain food to eat. The panda's generally calm nature and its diet of plants, rather than meat, established it long ago as a Chinese symbol of peace.

*An adult giant panda spends most of its life alone.*

# THE PANDA'S NEIGHBORHOOD

Researchers have tracked the movements of giant pandas by fitting them with radio collars. Giant pandas do most of their traveling in fairly private neighborhoods called **home ranges.** They seem to generally avoid each other by choice, rather than by driving other pandas away.

An adult panda spends most of its life alone. An obvious exception is a female panda with her **cub.** Another exception is during spring courtship, when adult male and female pandas seek each other's company. And at other times, pandas mingle briefly during squabbles over mates or territorial boundaries. In one unusual case, a Chinese researcher observed an adult male panda that allowed a young panda to follow him around.

Pandas often live in dense cover, so they cannot easily see one another. They communicate their presence by making **scent markings** and scrapes on tree trunks and stones. Scent markings are droppings, urine, or oil from anal sacs. They tell a panda passerby quite a bit, such as the gender and size of the panda that left the message.

A male panda's home range averages about 5 square miles (13 sq. km). A female's range is generally somewhat smaller than a male's. The home range of an adult panda usually overlaps part of at least one other panda's range. In one study area, adult male pandas had three to five females sharing at least part of their home range.

*Mist* (above) *and thick plant growth* (below) *make it hard for pandas to see one another from a distance.*

In some places, young males have the largest home ranges. That is because they tend to wander the farthest as they try to establish a home range near female pandas. A male panda is usually at least 8 years old before it can establish a home range overlapping the ranges of female pandas. Before age 8, a young male can be driven away by older males.

As male pandas age, they lose strength and energy. By about 15 years of age, male pandas are no longer in the prime of their lives. Younger males move in, and older males retreat to new, smaller ranges.

A panda's home range shifts somewhat with the seasons. From September to May, for example, pandas tend to occupy a winter range. The winter range is at a lower elevation than the summer range.

*Young male pandas tend to wander more than older pandas.*

*A mother panda and her 1-month-old baby*

## COURTSHIP AND CUBS

During the spring breeding season, the time when pandas mate, they make more scent markings. Pandas also communicate vocally more often during the breeding season, making a variety of moans, chirps, and barks.

Researchers have found that a female panda is probably interested in male pandas for little more than 1 week each spring. She may actually mate on only 2 or 3 days of that period. During that time, she may mate with more than one male. After each brief encounter, she and her mate have nothing to do with each other. Each panda goes its separate way. The father panda has no role in raising his offspring.

31

A female panda has a flexible **gestation period** that varies from 87 to 163 days. The gestation period is the length of time a baby develops in its mother's body before being born. After a panda's egg has been fertilized in her body, it floats freely for 1 to 4 months. Eventually, the egg attaches to the wall of the mother's uterus and develops into a panda cub.

The mother panda gives birth in a rock crevice, cave, or hollow tree. She bears one, two, or occasionally three cubs. If she has more than one cub, she usually raises only one. The mother panda takes one of the newborn cubs and holds it to her breast. She licks it and feeds it milk from her body almost nonstop. That maternal attention makes for one safe and healthy cub. But the mother panda generally ignores any additional cubs. They are left to starve. Why female pandas sometimes bear more than one cub, yet raise only one, is somewhat of a mystery. It may simply be nature's way of ensuring the survival of at least one cub.

*A giant panda cuddles her cub* (left) *and licks it to keep it clean* (above left).

Other than its instinctive abilities to **nurse,** or drink milk, and squawk, a panda cub is born quite helpless. The cub's eyes are closed, and it is nearly hairless. It weighs no more than a stick of butter, about 3 to 5 ounces (90-140 g). It takes as many as five newborn pandas to weigh 1 pound (0.5 kg)!

The mother panda stays with her cub for several days, perhaps as long as 1 month. She **fasts,** or goes without eating, during this time. It is a mystery how the mother panda can store enough energy on a bamboo diet to fast for several weeks while her cub grows. Finally, she breaks her fast and begins to eat again. During the next few months, the mother will leave the cub only to feed. When she is gone, the cub sleeps, saving its energy to nurse when its mother returns.

*A tiny panda cub can make a lot of noise!*

33

During its second month, the panda cub opens its eyes and begins to crawl. In its third month, the cub begins to walk and occasionally stand. The cub begins to leave its shelter and roam with its mother when it is between 4 and 5 months old. By then, the panda is the size of a typical house cat. It is about 16 inches (40 cm) long and weighs about 13 pounds (6 kg). The cub soon begins to sample bamboo. When the cub is 8 or 9 months old, its mother discourages it from nursing by pushing it away. That forces the cub to dine almost entirely on bamboo.

Giant panda cubs at 2 months (opposite page),
4 months (left), and 6 months (below) of age.

*Leopards sometimes kill giant panda cubs whose mothers are not nearby to protect them.*

The panda grows up under the watchful eye of its mother. The cub learns to drink from streams and climb trees, and it becomes familiar with the forest around it.

Panda cubs face dangers. A cub could be orphaned by the death of its mother, or it could be snatched by a predator. Yellow-throated martens and golden cats can kill small panda cubs that are not in their mother's care. Asiatic black bears and leopards can kill larger cubs. But predators are no threat to a full-grown female panda.

Panda cubs remain with their mothers until they are at least 18 months old. Occasionally a young panda stays with its mother until it is nearly 3 years old. When the mother panda is ready to mate again, she drives her cub away. The cub wanders some distance from its mother's home range, seeking a new home range of its own. Researchers know little about how juvenile pandas find home ranges for themselves.

By the age of 5 or 6, a cub reaches full size and is ready to mate. Pandas typically mate each year from the time of maturity until they are about 15. A captive giant panda in China, however, gave birth when she was 19. Wild pandas probably live 18 to 20 years, although one captive giant panda lived to be 34.

*A 1-year-old panda with its mother*

# SAVING THE GIANT PANDA

Until recent years, giant pandas were often the victims of hunters. Rural Chinese people have traditionally hunted all forest creatures for food. Pandas were especially valuable. Their fur could be sold, and their bones could be used in traditional Chinese medicine. But then the Chinese government made hunting giant pandas illegal. Anyone convicted of killing a panda can be sentenced to jail or even death. The new laws have eliminated most hunting. Giant pandas face greater challenges, however. Whether wild pandas will survive ultimately depends upon how China manages its natural resources and upon how much help it gets from the outside world.

China has over one billion people. Finding enough land on which people can live and raise crops is an ongoing problem. Over the centuries, villages have sprouted in many parts of the back country where pandas live. Forests have been cleared for farms and firewood. Panda habitat has shrunk. It has been broken into separate parcels, like a jigsaw puzzle scattered into pieces. Not until the late 1990s did the Chinese government show a serious willingness to protect remaining panda habitat from tree cutters.

Unlike the United States or Canada, China does not have a tradition of wildlife protection and national parks. The idea of saving land for the benefit of wild animals is new to China. But in 1998, the government announced a nationwide logging ban to protect forests and prevent erosion. Time will tell whether the ban will be enforced successfully.

Even if the forests begin to grow back, the wild panda population will be safe only if pandas from one region can reach pandas in another. In the long term, a group of animals stays healthy only if it has new animals from outside the family with which to mate and produce offspring. Otherwise, the related animals living in an area breed only among themselves. That can result in what scientists call **inbreeding.** Over time, inbreeding causes physical flaws, such as an inability to have young, to become more and more common within a group of animals.

**Above:** *Chinese people cut trees to get firewood to cook their food.*
**Opposite page:** *Many forests that were good habitat for giant pandas have been cut down to make room for farms.*

The surviving panda groups do not show signs of inbreeding yet. But inbreeding may become a problem, unless the reserves can be strung together like beads. This would allow pandas to travel between the reserves. As it is, the groups of pandas are more or less isolated. Each reserve is like an island, cut off from the others by bare hillsides and growing villages. Pandas in one region cannot reach pandas in another region.

The Chinese government's "Grain to Green" policy is designed to restore forests on hillsides where all of the trees have been cut down. Programs like Grain to Green may be able to restore forests that would bridge the gaps between panda reserves. Whether or not the government will commit enough money and energy to make the plan successful remains to be seen. China's population continues to grow. Saving huge tracts of trees for animals is a challenge.

*Farms covering a mountainside can keep giant pandas from traveling between patches of forest.*

One way to increase both the numbers and the diversity of pandas would be to release unrelated, captive-born animals into the wild. But giant pandas are scarce even in captivity.

Chinese researchers are breeding captive pandas to increase the population. When a captive panda gives birth to twins and abandons one of the cubs, scientists try to raise the abandoned baby. But it is difficult for humans to raise baby pandas. The cubs have trouble digesting food other than panda milk. In 1999, Mark Edwards, chief nutritionist (animal feeding specialist) at the San Diego Zoo, developed a panda baby food. It is a mixture of human infant formula and a milk substitute used for feeding puppies. The mixture is enough like panda milk that it is easy for a baby panda to digest. This promising new food has raised hopes that more baby pandas can be reared successfully.

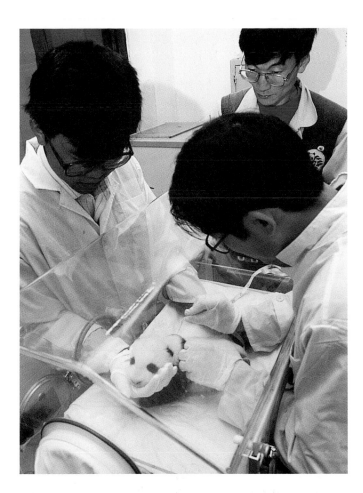

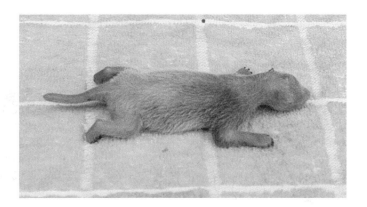

**Left:** *A newborn panda at a captive breeding center*
**Above:** *A baby panda in an incubator*
**Top:** *Scientists give a giant panda cub a medical examination.*

Even if more captive pandas become available, there may not be suitable places to release them. Until Chinese scientists and the Chinese government believe that any of the existing wild habitats is truly safe for additional pandas, they will not release them. No one knows if or when that will happen. And some people wonder if the Chinese government truly wants to return captive-bred pandas to the wild.

Why would the Chinese *not* want to release pandas? If you raised rare geese that laid golden eggs, would you return the geese to the wild? For the Chinese,

pandas may be something like those geese. China can rent a pair of pandas to a zoo in a foreign country for about $100,000 per month. That is good for the people who rent pandas and for the ones who love to watch pandas. But is it good for pandas?

Money earned from the rent-a-panda program is supposed to be used to improve panda **conservation programs,** or programs that protect wild pandas. And China insists that zoos exhibiting pandas must pay for scientists to study those pandas in the hopes of improving panda conservation.

Some Western countries and wildlife organizations have criticized China for spending money on captive breeding while ignoring the desperate needs of wild pandas. Western conservationists have traditionally believed that the survival of *wild* pandas is what is most important. The main goal of captive breeding, they say, should be to restock the wild population, not to restock zoos. At least captive breeding reduces the need to capture even more wild pandas for zoo exhibits.

The heart of China's captive breeding program is the China Conservation and Research Center for the Giant Panda, or CCRC. The CCRC lies within the Wolong Nature Reserve (see map, page 17), along the rushing Pitiao River in northwest Sichuan Province. It is nestled in a valley guarded by rocky peaks. The center was founded in 1980 by the Chinese government and the World Wildlife Fund. It is the largest and most successful captive breeding site for pandas. Some zoos have had success in breeding pandas, but not as much as the CCRC has had. In recent years, the CCRC has produced several baby pandas annually.

The CCRC is something of a panda hotel, nursery, and retirement village. The 45 or so pandas living there enjoy exercise yards, private quarters, and the close attention of the CCRC staff and researchers from many countries. Elsewhere, Chinese zoos have about 65 more captive pandas. Another dozen or so live in zoos outside China.

**Above:** *Wolong Panda Reserve, Sichuan, China*
**Left:** *A worker gathers bamboo to feed captive pandas.*

*If it is to survive, the giant panda needs the help of people around the world.*

Some Chinese people seem to agree with Western conservationists that the bamboo bear and its habitat are well worth saving. The giant panda lives in the most biologically rich temperate forest on earth. At the Wolong Reserve, for example, scientists have cataloged an amazing number of plants and animals: 4,000 plants, 1,700 insects, and 450 **vertebrates**—various fish, **amphibians,** reptiles, birds, and mammals.

The Chinese call their giant pandas a national treasure. But pandas are more than that. They are one of the planet's treasures. Fittingly enough, the panda's fate depends on the world, not just the people of China. Captive breeding research and facilities, land protection, education, and law enforcement are costly. China cannot, or will not, shoulder all the costs. Saving wild pandas will take creativity, generosity, and the committed goodwill of many organizations and individuals. Then, perhaps, this most unusual of bears will forever romp and roll among the wild, green gardens of bamboo.

# GLOSSARY

**amphibians:** animals that have lungs as adults but begin life in water as tadpoles with gills

**bamboo:** a hard-stemmed grass that is the giant panda's main food

**bamboo crashes:** the dying off of huge tracts of bamboo at one time, after the plants have bloomed

**carnivores:** meat-eating animals

**carrion:** the rotting flesh of dead animals

**conservation programs:** programs that protect wild animals

**cub:** a baby giant panda

**digit:** a finger or toe

**DNA:** the material in the cells of living things that passes characteristics from parents to their offspring

**elevations:** heights above sea level

**endangered:** in danger of dying off

**fasts:** goes without eating

**gestation period:** the length of time a baby develops in its mother's body before being born

**habitat:** the place where an animal normally lives

**hibernate:** to spend the winter in a sleeplike state in which an animal's body systems slow dramatically

**home ranges:** areas in which individual giant pandas live

**inbreeding:** an increase in the number of physical flaws in a population of related animals that breed only among themselves

**lichens:** plants that look like dry moss

**mammal:** an animal that feeds its young with milk from the mother's body

**muzzle:** the mouth, nose, and jaws of an animal

**nurse:** to drink mother's milk

**predators:** animals that hunt and eat other animals

**reserves:** places where animals are protected

**scent markings:** droppings, urine, or oil from anal sacs that a giant panda leaves on tree trunks or stones to tell other pandas of its presence

**species:** a group of plants or animals that are alike in certain ways

**taxonomists:** scientists who classify animals into groups based on how they are related to one another

**temperate:** neither very hot nor very cold

**vertebrates:** animals with backbones

# INDEX

# ABOUT THE AUTHOR

**Lynn M. Stone** is an author and wildlife photographer who has written more than 400 books for young readers about wildlife and natural history. Mr. Stone enjoys fishing, travel, and photographing wildlife. He is a former teacher and lives with his family in St. Charles, Illinois.

# ABOUT THE PHOTOGRAPHER

**Keren Su** was born in Hangzhou, China. He is a self-taught painter, photographer, adventurer, and culture explorer. Keren has published written and photographic accounts of the lives of Chinese minority peoples, sharing glimpses of many never-before-seen parts of China and the people who live there. He has received numerous awards for his photography of people and nature.

48

Westfield Memorial Library
Westfield, New Jersey